Prelude to Passion
Journey of Love

Maureen McCarthy

St. Bede's Publications
Petersham, Massachusetts

Illustrations by the author

LC Number: 98-61709

ISBN 1-879007-36-3

Published by: St. Bede's Publications
              P. O. Box 545
              Petersham, Massachusetts 01366

Contents

*This book is dedicated lovingly to
my husband, Eugene.
It is all that I can give,
a token.
And to all the friends,
relatives, colleagues, neighbors,
fellow-sufferers in hospitals;
in fact, to all those who continue
to seek with us
the life of the spirit and pursue
the journey toward passion*

Introduction

Each of us makes a journey. Some experience hardships and suffering along the way. All, however, encounter some adversity as well as joy in some form or other as that is the nature of life. This collection of poems concentrates on our own personal journeys toward love and ultimately what becomes our passion.

In July 1995, when I was first diagnosed with a rare and highly malignant cancer, my journey became clearly defined. With the information, I was able to recognize what was to be my special road; the unique character of my personal passion.

The battle with the disease altered the journey for me and for my family. When I first learned the news, I likened it to a rogue wave rising menacingly from the sea, unanticipated, destroying all in its path. That concept is a focus for the chapter in this book which contains the poems conceived during the early stages of what became a savage approach to treatment and is titled *Rogue Wave*.

Since the journey is filled with light as well as shadows, the rest of the book represents insights about family and traditions; childhood memories; nostalgia for things and people who are gone from my experience. In *Under the Rainbow*, the poems were specifically created for family members or close friends, as in "La Meta," and "The Talisman"; or were to celebrate some particular event, as in "Daisy Chain," written for the funeral of my mother-in-law in November 1997. "Renewal" celebrates my own fortieth wedding anniversary.

Spirit Dances calls more emphatically to us to energize the spiritual life, locating "the spirit that dwells within" for each of us.

In the group entitled *Love Songs*, I tried to collect those poems which explore the joy of both human and divine love, the experience of complete union, and the growth of that love as we continue the journey.

Heart Beats, the closing chapter, is a more eclectic gathering of pieces of nostalgia containing memories of special events and people with whom I have shared intimately the passion and the journey.

Often I have been asked not only why I write, but how I write these poems. Most of them are from entries in a personal journal, a practice I find enormously helpful. Others are a "dancing spirit" that can enter my heart at any time and get scribbled on whatever is handy. Most of all, I try to keep the following self-instruction in mind and I beg you to keep these phrases in mind as you wander through the *Prelude to Passion*, and share in the *Journey of Love* with me. Enter into communication with your own spirit and know you have shared intimately with mine.

> Remember that my songs are prayers,
> So pray first.
> Offer the effort, the work, to God.
> Then let the words paint out the picture
> Which is bursting through the heart,
> Tumbling down the long white page.

October 1998
New York City

Acknowledgments

Any undertaking like the production of a book cannot be accomplished without many selfless contributions from many sources. As is the case with *Prelude to Passion*, the burden has been shared by countless people, some of whom remain unaware of how significant a contribution they made to my endeavors. I am deeply grateful to all of them and hesitate to mention specific names, fearing injury of oversight to all the others.

However, there are a few individuals whose assistance was so timely or so continual that they must be cited. Encouragement, hope when I needed it most, and eventual endorsement is the gift of Gerald O'Collins, S.J. of the Gregorian University. I owe also the introduction to the area of Barrea and the mountain called La Meta to Fred Brenk, S.J. of the Biblical Institute. Both of these men live and teach in Rome and represent communities on which my husband and I depend heavily for spiritual nourishment.

Reproduction techniques, collation, typing and transcribing were the shared effort of a truly great team of friends: Tatiana Ayuso, Norma Moshiem, and Lucia Paolise.

This work has been strongly influenced by my struggle with cancer, and so it is important to me that I acknowledge my enormous gratitude to the staff and doctors of the institutions responsible for my care: at St. Vincent's Cancer Care Center in New York, to their nursing staff and especially with love to Gerald Rosen, M.D., my oncologist; at Memorial Sloan Kettering in New York to their staff and to my surgeons, Mamjet Bains, M.D., Patrick

Boland, M.D., and posthumously to Michael Burt, M.D. and to the oncology team headed by Gary Schwartz, M.D.

I have spent so much time over the last two years at these marvelous care facilities that they have become more than hospitals to me; they have kept me alive and healthy. I also must mention the very unique and loving care and support that has been given to my husband and myself by Thomas Fahey, M.D. the Director of Memorial Sloan Kettering.

Friends, family, associates have always been ready with generous spirit to give support, encouragement and strength—often just the peace of being there with their love at the most critical times.

Without our spiritual communities, which is a large network including groups of dedicated religious, missionaries, and lay apostolates, we could not continue to sustain this battle. To all of you, everywhere, my thanks!

Under the Rainbow

Flowers for Charlie
(Dedicated to Charles Rich)

I did not see necessarily
    That poetry could be alive
    In my few lines of scrawl;
That songs could rise from any page;
But Charlie would have none of my objections.

He had a faith, a power,
    To overcome my pride,
    My self-obsession.
    I wore it as adornment,
Perhaps to hide my vanity.

At his insistence,
    With such careful nourishment
    Of the weakness in my soul,
    The flowers, as he called them,
Finally blossomed.

They were massed in a collection;
    Neat little rows
    Bursting with mystery
Of heart contemplating heart.

Each time I review them
    Charlie sits nearby,
    Quietly, unequivocally urging
That I believe again in me.

To taste the gift of faith,
    Is to remember that shared fragments
    Of my soul will eventually return,
Making all my smallness whole.

Love's Longing

The camellias have gone,
    All cut down.
The banyan tree looms
    With empty arms
So sadly at my doorway.

No more shrill cries from my little one,
    Seeking her favorite salamander
        Playmate.
The empty day stretches lonely arms
        Before me;
My heart cries with the pain of loss.

Each departure now becomes
    More wrenching,
    More poignant.
    Time has already run the distance
And I cannot undo a single day;
    A simple moment stop.

All is left are memories
    Why are they so bittersweet?

Tropical Dreams

Banyan branches dance
   Their mesmerizing pace
To silent rhythms
   Only they can hear.

Hibiscus bloom
   Ecstatically aware,
That their day
   Will be important
And their short but brilliant life.

Gardenia trees are sprouting
   Surprised at their exquisiteness
The perfection of their creamy white
   The headliners of perfume.

Sunflower Time

This is sunflower time;
    Standing tall they bear
The heat of the day,
The scorn of the cool nights,
Just turning toward the sun.

Uplifting arms and hearts and self
    So mightily that even
    Strong September winds cannot
Take them down.
Truly, this is a sunflower time.

Renewal

We learn to believe again
  In the impossible
To trust again that choices
  Are inspired;
That what was once delightful
  To our lusty youth
Is still the goodness of the
  Heart's desire.

This lovely day what can we give
  But to each other our very selves,
That gift which above all else glows
  Defined within the scrutinous glance.
We appreciate that without the lover,
  Without that praise or gentle supervision
We are the tinkling cymbals of cliché.

Each time we miss an opportunity to grow
  We feel uprooted,
Yet each year in spite of what we are
  Rings are added to the tree.
We locate self inside the other,
  That object of our life-long search.
In the dreary details we are surprised
  To see it blooming everywhere
From the distant hill we see so clearly
  The aspects of a love grown quite divine.
As with the Cana wedding feast
  The best is last
And now we taste the wine.

A Daisy Chain for Departure Day

Unfinished novels lay in bottom drawers
Swaddled in their bands of string,
Waiting for a lifetime rest.
The Dickens served so well the mechanism
Of companion, escape, precursor to each birth.

In all the living there appeared
An acquiescent nod to plans not hers,
In times not of her choosing,
Murmuring the inevitable response,
Acknowledging a will beyond her wishing.

Mary's gestures implied in every move
Scars of wounds beyond the telling;
All wisdom's gentle secrets gleaming in the smile
Reserved until a child unlocked its sentence.

An intellect that simplified with purpose.
Challenged all to seek a higher state,
But could achieve her purpose all too swiftly
Premonition never being duped
Or plans suspect.

A life of all the pieces of the living,
Joy and sorrow interstitially infused,
Redemptive grace a candle flame to light the path
For children and their children;
Love's daisy chain for all the generations.

"Look down on us our gentle Mother,
We have placed all our hope in you."

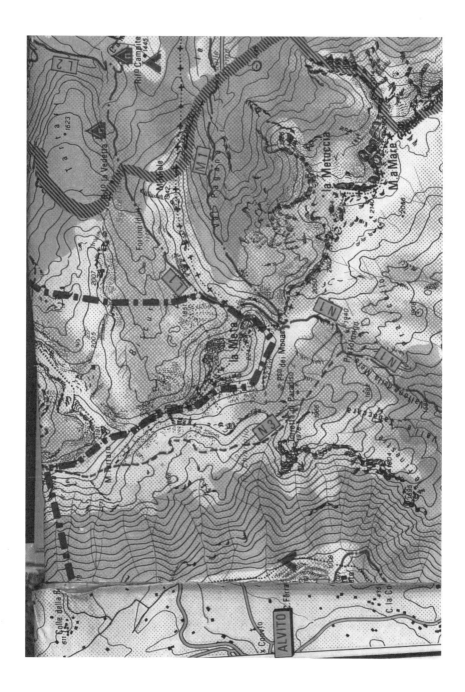

La Meta

Heralding this welcome landmark
  We witness our passage.
In past and present to reminisce,
  Shaping our memories to fit this space
    Of gains and losses,
      Of victories and crosses,
        Goals, accomplishments and
Call on them now in Peace.

Transparencies in candlelight take shape.
  Life's faces are lifted once more.
Unmasking some shadows in each little life,
  Speaking of what I possess;
An outrageously generous love gift
  They are mine.
My cymbals crashing.
  My lamps burning,
    My trumpets blaring,
Sing proudly new of Hope.

My life's companions, tonight you shine
  In every corner of my heart.
To demonstrate what yesterday
  Could not hold.
You are my measure
  Poured out from God's sleeve,
    That part of His love He calls.
      Me.

*La Meta is a mountain in the Barrea section of Italy. It means "the goal." Climbers use it as a measure of their skills.

11

The Talisman

I

He prayed. She prayed.
   Alone, together, constantly,
Begging in unity a sign
   To show them what to choose
Of life's exciting ways.

They vowed to each other a life
   No longer separate;
And promised God to always,
   Forever do his will.

Sacrifices came with love,
   First one and then the other.
Surely now they would discover
   What it was that could be done.

The years bundled into decades
   Seeking joy in others' faces,
Being joy in all the places they could fill;
   Speaking to the one who understood
That they still sought to do his will.

II

It happened in November that a warm breeze
    Fluttered at the drapery in the drawing room.
She heard it, he heard it;
    It made their beating hearts
    Stand absolutely still.

"I give you now my talisman,
    Symbol of my love to celebrate
What you have done for me;
    My lovely ones, you are my hands, my heart.

Mending what is torn with grief,
    Bonding yourselves to all the weak,
All the fragile ones who need your strength.

You stitch up all the broken ones
    The world has torn apart,
Without ever asking why you always do my will.
    You live my love in perfect love with me."

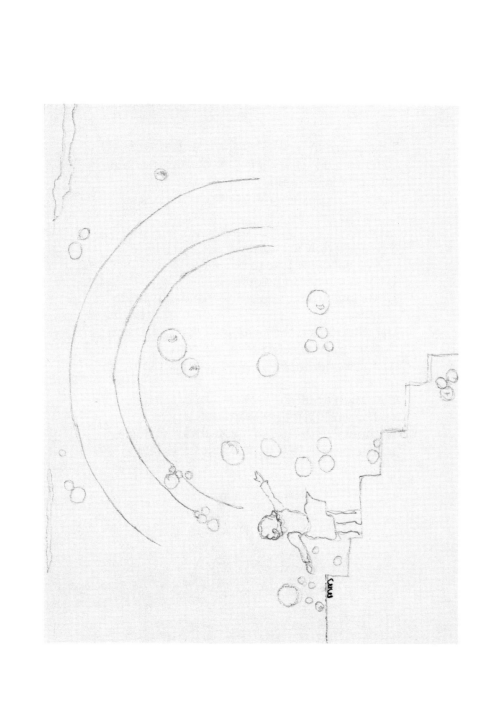

Barley Moon

Once each year September comes striding in
    With white-capped tides
All the ocean tries to climb upon the land;
    The tree limbs bow,
  Flowers fray from huddled plants.
  The sequence of time stands still.
The season as we know it stops to shout,
"Please stay, be mine, I love your warmth.
  Your sunny summer glances."
Careless of the precious days we spent it all.
  The darkness becomes a floodlit stage
    To play out nostalgia's fancy
  For all the years we had to celebrate;
  To watch our children come and go;
  To now see children's children dance
    In the light of our barley moon.

Winter Solstice

I

When autumn changes clothes,
Winter comes colliding with the Christmas feast,
Moving on to dreary January
    Heralding the great tradition
    Of the gathering of the clan.

Our hobbled steeds wait patiently
    In barren woodlands,
    Lively withers shaking in the cold,
Golden livery flashes, lighting icy puddles in the snow;
    Chasing out the twinkling moonbeam glow.
The shadows dance a jig against the firelight,
    Silhouetting faces we all know.

II

We have come again from valleys distant,
    Across our fields and theirs;
    Some up from the sea,
On this ancient hill to cheer, to dance, to celebrate,
Renewal of a pride, rebirth of our new year;
Paying honor solemnly
    To all those who wait above the stars;
We demonstrate that family
Through centuries of love and sacrifice,
    Can stir desire in the soul to more beyond this life.

We energize the young,
    Encourage hope for all the old;
But most of all we venerate
    The moment of the now.

Rogue Wave

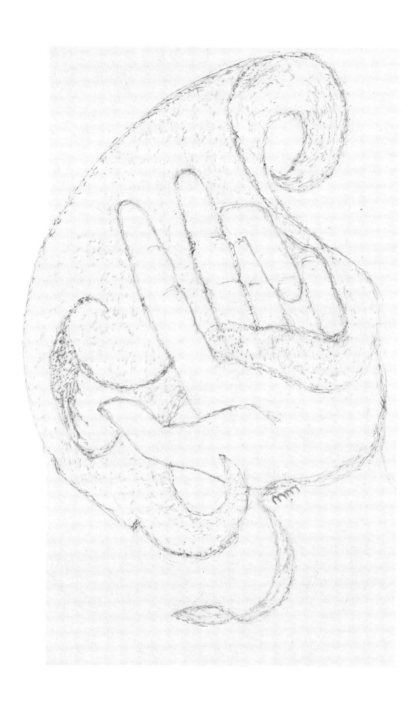

Banners in the Sunset

The anguish of the heavy heart
    Sorrowing beyond belief,
    At the chastisement.

The pain of becoming the penitent,
    So fearful,
    So frightened;
Bewildered by the retribution required,
Knowing only how to love,
    To celebrate the other,
    To live in daily hope.

We beg sincerely
    In vanity demand
    A symbol
    A banner for fidelity.

When reality inscribed
    With stunning certainty
    Stills the heart
    Stealing all the air
    From every corner of the room
To see beyond a doubting instant
    Our banner flies
    Searing the sky with blood
    Crimson of the passion
    Scarlet for the pain.

Secrets

I

There is a certain sweetness
        To foreknowledge
To see a privileged piece
        Of your reality,
The first inkling that you are carrying
        The perfect seed of life;
An approaching miracle.

So lovely is that first instant,
        Being able to savor the reality,
Independent of any reinforcement.
Somehow sharing the knowledge,
        Even with loved ones,
Does not outweigh a need
        To stand back for a look at it;
Savor the unique ownership
        Of this moment, this truth.

II

But to live in community
    We must share,
The shared experience becomes
    Our sacrament.
So you finally tell the secret
    And you know that by the act
You have given up the right to own it.

    You lose the priority on truth
But you must do it to survive
    The burden of this truth.

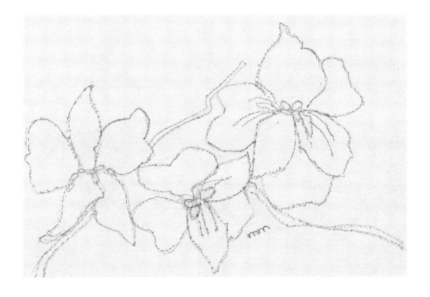

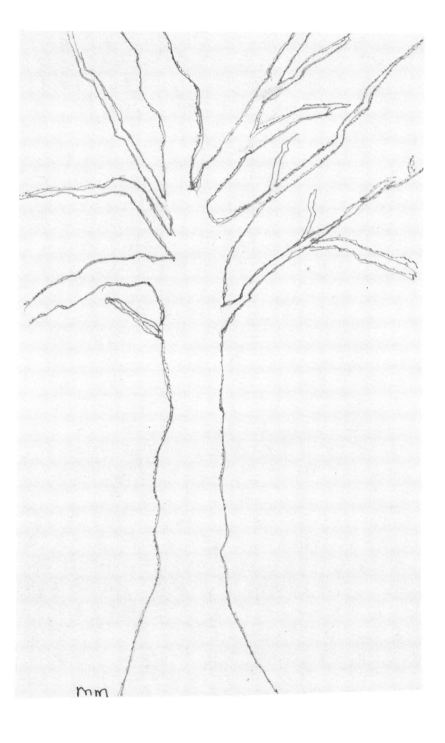

mm

To Live in Broken Pieces

It takes time to mend.
  Time to fix;
To build the bridges
To inspire confidence.

When will I become believable?
  I wait for them to trust me.
What if they do not, cannot, or
  Will not?
What if my experience
All this pain cannot be shared?

  That is acceptable too,
The time for healing takes
More energy than I can muster.

The broken pieces of my body
The painful corners of my heart
  Are waiting quietly to mend,
  In between the spaces,
In between those darkest places,
    I AM!

Sacrifice

Distended stomachs
      Amputated limbs
Gurgles and gasps
      Is that all there is?

Look into the faces
      Study those eyes
Encased in their circles of gray.

There is the meaning
      There is the reason
There is my moment's being.

But can I do this
      Do I want this
How can I escape?

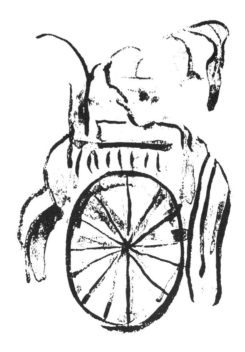

Baldness

Invasion of body,
Invasion of spirit,
When there is nothing to do but wait.

True dependence,
Ultimate will;
Trust is the only factor left,
The ultimate directionless space.

Trust does not go anywhere,
Does not lead to anything,
But demands a resting heart.

It needs a spirit
That has sublimated will
To sure knowledge;
To the opening sounds of the song,
The sound of the wings of hope.

Battle Cry

I

In a journey that has been
     As much in darkness
     As in light,
You have been with me
     Helping me see
Sunsets fading,
     Fireworks at sea,
Tree lines below snow caps
     Mountain tops above the clouds.
You have shown them to me
As to a wondering, skeptical child
     Striding through life.

II

In the struggles on the hill
     Where pain surrounds,
     Smothers and we blindly grope,
You are my guide,
     Support and comforter
Calming fears,
Soothing pain,
Nourishing the child in me.

In the silence of my heart
     That is as much a prayer,
You are in me,
     Holding me fast,
Giving me the courage,
     The adventure of hope
Keeping us both alive!

The Winding Sheet

It is powerful
   This feeling of awe,
Knowing that I can recognize
   In them a depth of pain.

Pain I have not yet reached,
   I cannot really see;
   But somehow feel
As viscerally tangible
   As the wrapping of a shroud.

Christmas Day

More than acceptance
    Is my wish
More than blind toleration
    Is my goal.

I want to take up this
    Weighty burden
To wear it constantly,
    So constantly that I may learn
        Its fashion.

Doubtless it will fashion me
    In a way that clothes will often do,
Disguising the figure,
    The faults.

Perhaps it will free me
    From constraints of a previous day.

Some synthetic delusions
    To conformity
Give back the reflection,
    The unique interpretation of this reality.

Instead of mirroring the image
    It permits a new creation
    All around me
Instead of living inside it,
    I choose to live through it.

Cleaning Closets

There they hang
    Vestigial fragments of a life
Lived with ferocity,
    Such delicious joy,
    Such agonizing sorrows.

There's the jacket I grabbed the morning
    I lost my son,
Saying as I did it,
    "God wouldn't let this happen."

Perhaps I keep it to remind myself
    God does let life happen
Death, understandings, pain
    Are part of that process of life.

The suit we bought in Paris
    So daring,
    So chic.
The room comes alive again
    With the lively exchange between
    You, my darling, and the ever so Parisienne
        salesclerk.

The exhilaration still fills me with joy.
Perhaps that's why I kept it
To remind me of all my joys.

The ball dresses stand guard
Patiently, limply
Waiting to be warm and wonderfully
Alive.

All of them favorites for so many
Of my dashing nights.
Yes that was a time of splendid fun
Enjoyment in all things

And now they wait for me again
To tell of their future.

The Spirit with Hot Chocolate

Once again I am awakened
By the body's needs.
Sometimes they complain separately
This morning furious at having been ignored
so long,
They scream in unison for attention.

They are really so very physical,
But my treatment for them is swift and simple,
The bones and joints want their share of love and
affection
For them the task is motion

The stubborn bowels make undignified sounds
Alarm systems are malfunctioning.
To them I give a warning
Here is the time and the place for disgrace
Better now or never!

To the stomach that moans for a morsel or two
I give a hot chocolate for solace
For the needles and pins on a scalp
That is fighting to keep some hair
I finally attend with an ice bag
I wonder what else I have forgotten.

Ah, the spirit complains
It has been lost in the shuffle
In all the sounds of the jungle.
So I reach for my pen,
Open the cage,
And marvel at its splendor.

Sea Change: Los Desapparisidos

That is where I am all ready,
        Lost among the missing ones.
I was not ready, Oh, Lord, was I
        To disappear so soon?

Insidiously it begins,
        Not being able to be
In the reality of yesterday
        Which gave me my identity.

Calendar deadlines vanish one by one,
        Activities and invitations,
The structure and form are past tense now.

Hairdresser and gym are frivolous pursuits
        Have not been attended in over a year.
Even shopping for groceries has become an event.

It takes my breath away,
        To be overtaken by this change so quickly.
There are still some resting places,
        In the valleys between the hills.

That little spark of hope keeps me fighting,
        Will keep me alive,
A mere penny candle casting shadows on the wall,
        It announces to my world
I have not disappeared quite yet!

Beginnings

Telling such a secret
    Is the hardest part of all
To those you love
    And who love you beyond measure.

It is the first of all
    The many sacrifices
The first pain among so many
    The first inspiration
To make the journey for them.

Spirit Dances

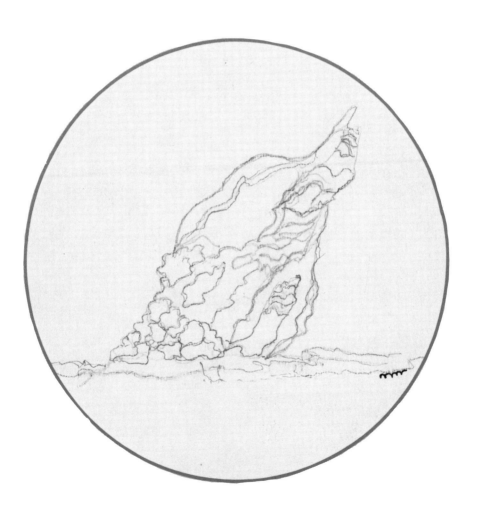

Millennium

I am a star,
    Gleaming,
In the millionth year
    Of a millionth night
    Alone.

I am a shadow,
    Lengthened,
To cover the vastness
    Of desert infinity,
    Silent.

I am a wounded child,
    Resting,
Peaceful in the folds
    Of a Father's arms;
    Asleep.

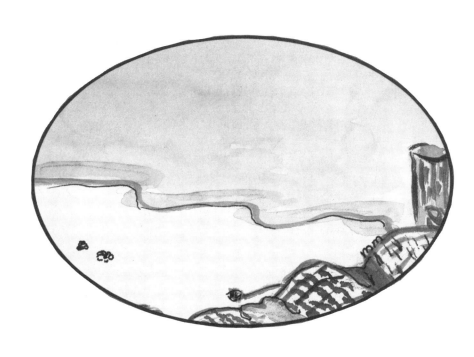

Stone in a Still Pond

The stone in the pool,
    Ring upon ring,
From you to me and beyond.
In the dearest circle of love,
    Mother, father, all generations,
All friends and associates,
    To me.

To experience the Eucharist
    That assumes the essential you;
You are the Christ,
    But you are also all of them,
    In me.

Oh the sweetness of this possibility,
    To unite again in this communion;
More than spirit,
More than flesh,
More than circles in circles;
    All circles are one.

Heart Whispers

The power of the Spirit
　　Impresses itself on me.
It catches at my soul,
　　Flashes into my heart;
It captures my awareness.
Suddenly, I realize what I never knew,
　　The thought and wish,
　　Truly desired,
　　Authentically good,
Eventually becomes my reality.

Purpose

There is no
　　Should have been.
There is only
　　What might have been.
There is only
　　Now and here.
This is the lesson
　　That lives in the why.

Finding the Center

I

The call comes unexpectedly
The mind forgets to interfere
    All muscles, nervous limbs
            and light
Fall inward.

Bending, weaving concave slopes
    Gently carving an altered heart
Becoming each other's walls
The fire begins to grow
In the darkness
You are everywhere
        In me.

II

Gently centering
Each wall melts to share
        In singleness of purpose.

Fire begins from coals
    Last night's heat
Growing in the dark
    Everywhere there are you
            In every part of me.

School Day

Oh, Mother Wisdom,
What must I do
To learn the ways of love,
To make it all come true?

My child, it is no simple lesson
Learned from any book.
Take the path of knowledge and expression
The one which Jesus took.

The way is rough,
Clouded in confusion.
Remember who you are,
Keep some sentiment and illusion.

Be the object of a love,
So great it cannot fill a measure,
Use your capacity to serve the other,
It has become your treasure.

Epiphany

Time becomes so important
Each moment has its own personality.
Colors, tasks, pleasures to the senses
Bloom on greedy vines
Supported by the frame of their desire.

We don patience as an old familiar sweater
Reveling in its remembered comfort
Knowing that haste
Can chase away the goodness of the now.

Prayer at the End of the Day

Our spirits are breaking,
    The wine pouring out.
Give us, O Lord,
    Your hand.

Love Songs

Retrospect

Eager lover,
Broken body,
    Flesh with blood,
Given in love
    To me.

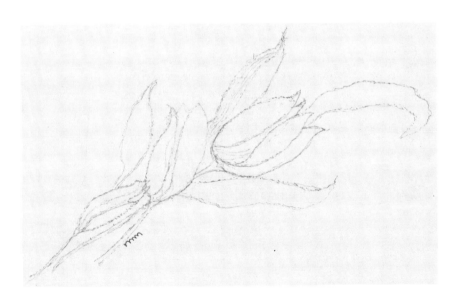

The Gift

You are fire
Keeping me warm, free from harm
   Protected from winter's chill

You feed me whitest wheat
Wrapping me in confidence and mist

You are light
When darkness approaches
The newborn mewling, whimpering
Inadequate: helpless to the last

Can it be that this delights you
The smile I feel that is your joy
   Pleasure in the pleasuring
Calming, comforting the lame and sore,
Your need has long been secret to me
   The want filled by my emptiness

Let it be that I may never grow
   Too strong, too vital, too informed
To leave the shelter of your embrace
   Or find success apart from
   My home within your hand.

With Sighs Too Deep for Words

Oh, Lord, how can I do the work to be done
    When activities increase daily?
It seems so unjust
That when at last I have a signal of your love for me
    The pressures of life increase
To make it impossible
    To do exactly what I know I must do.

In prayer you are leading me
    Closer each day.
That too takes time
I trust you and I love you,
    Offering this ultimate frustration to you,
Knowing that the anxiety of it all
    Is making it a dearer gift.

Thank you for making it so rare;
If the work goes too well
    Or costs less to give
The gifts will be less lovely.

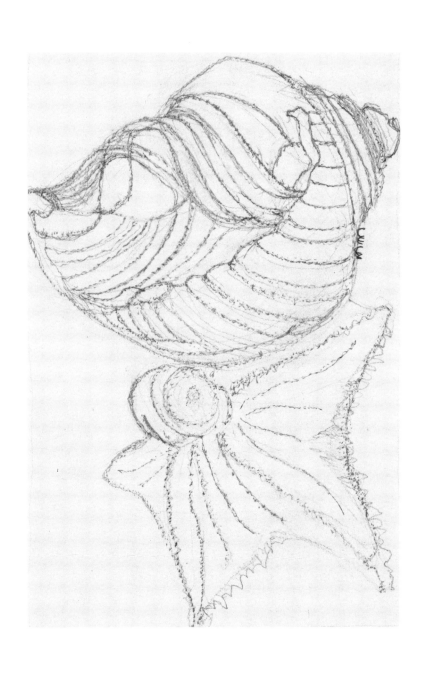

Discovery

Deeply from the mountain core
    Living in the mists
    Of vapors left
    By scudding, bumping clouds,

Surges a need, a will,
    With strength to fill
    The voids of all eternity.

I too am needing
    Beyond the measurable limit,
To fill the spaces;
    The core of you to shroud

To shield, envelop and sustain
    Is my sole purpose now
My strength has a mountain's durability.

The Gardener at Sunset

The lights still shine in Livingston,
    Although the gardener is at rest.
Fish ponds are stocked for spring
    With aimless carp who try to catch
The last few rays of light.

Hemlock hedges wall in the last of day,
    Darkening the rolling lawns.
Giant rhododendron trees march up the hill,
    Lifting heavy blossomed heads,
Reflecting rainbow hues against an indifferent sky.

A thousand daffodils tumble down the meadow
    Swaying to the evening breeze,
Trying to see if cowslip and the trillium
    Have finished laying carpets for the trees.

Now is the hour the statues claim their right to roam
    To mutely gaze at changes to their garden home
To peek at cloistered apple orchards
    Where blossom carpets dust their feet.

The gardener lifts his faded hat
    To better mount conservatory stairs
Where a more exotic garden needs his care,
    Too delicate are they for spring's night air.

Ceiling, walls, and floor will spring to life,
    Orchids turn to greet the last of day.
Up and down the rows of plants,
    He visits every one,
Reminding him of where they first had met;
    The Himalayas, China and Tibet.

He settles in the rocking chair beside them,
   To watch advancing shades of night.
Straw hat and pen in hand
   He writes the lengthy list;
The duties for tomorrow's brand new day.

Awake at Last

In your embrace this morning
    I can never remember such rapture,
Giving as I could my all,
    My everything.
From the depth and breadth
    All of him, all to him
    All because of him.

Is it possible that in the way
    Relationships evolve
It is only in the knowing
    Of the loss
That we can afford to empty ourselves
    To the other

Can it be that I have always
    Held a little of myself apart;
Or is it more likely that now
    There is more,
    So much more to give.

The Kiss

It arose from reverie
  I suppose
Longing for a time in history,
  A time of innocence,
  A romance of spirit.

In that moment was born the desire
  It would not be denied
  Now that it was acknowledged.

The inclination to deny the possible,
  To feel absurd in hope,
Inspired prayerful trust.
Relinquishing hope
  Made room for peace

So placing my desire
  In another woman's hands,
I moved to greet the lover
  To my astonishment
  Who bestowed the gift
Making all desire
  A sweet reality.

Christmas Song

Just as I woke to see
    That dark had not accomplished
    The important job of solace,
    Of comforting and healing,
My mind is clear,
    Tumbling about with
    Restless open phrases;
Desiring to speak of what I see,
    To share the beauty
    Of a new direction.

Early on this birthday morn,
    Is when I know so
    Unmistakably
That intimacy is shared,
The coming dawn is heralded
    By two or three;
    Not one
That you are there completely,
    Praying, thinking,
    Loving me;
Infusing me with gentle light.

II

I follow the glow
Above the peace of heart
    Which grows within,
Down to the smallest space,
    And instead of you,
    I discover me.

Heart Beats

Quilt Patterns

Some memories are for the future,
    The sentinels who stand and watch
Until called forth
To shore up flagging courage,
To soothe a troubled conscience,
    Or return the presence
Of someone who has gone.

Lessons are stored up
    For future need.
They jostle for a place in line,
Quite satisfied to stay
Until called;
Not struggling to rise
    Until the need.

We are so consoled
    To have them handy
The fabric of life's
    Own quilt
Each pattern teaches brand new reasons
    For making memories that stay.

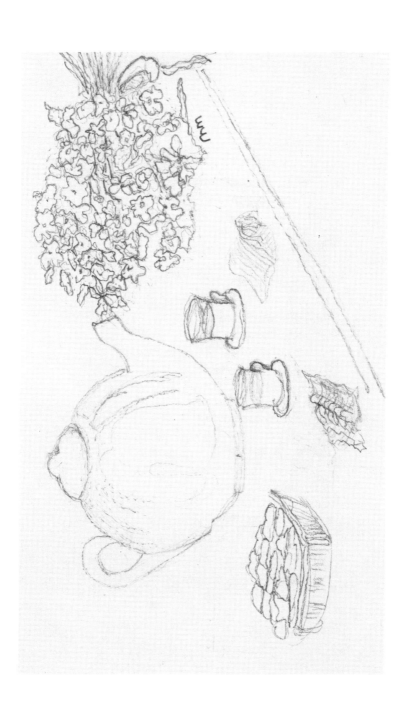

Bohemians in Gray

Living a truly monastic life,
Devoid of distractions,
Nothing personal or lavish
To take the eye
To distract the mind

Only two cups had they,
Yet all the teas
In all the world
Would never taste as sweet
As one we had last spring
With the Bishop and his wife
Who lived on Via Pie de Marmon.

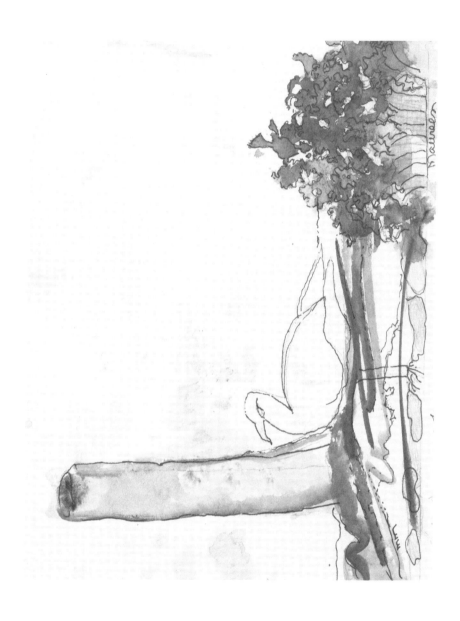

East River

Today you push along
   Stumbling over your ice chunks
Insisting yourself steadily
   Toward the sea.

I could not know this morning
How weighty the day would be
   The dreaded truth
   With simple message
Turns invincibility to vapor
The heart is filled with ice
   As mighty as your own.

Oh, tell me, Lady River,
   Through all ages still a friend
Why is it only in this stunning news
   Can I appreciate my love
So I could wish to have
   The awful burden
To save her in a plan
   Not mine, but yours.

To leave her with her family
   Her friends, her loves,
To take me instead
So sweet, bittersweet,
   To know how deep my love.

Overheard at Jackson Hole

A pair of pigtailed jumpers
      With knee socks and roller blades
And back packs that could have made Everest

"That lady over there is sick,
She used to come here often.
Let's ask Sister to pray for her
      Today and every day
So she is sure to get better."

What a beautiful prayer
What a lovely gift
My childhood stands there
Efficiently dealing with
      All my reality.

On Occasion of Meeting

Are we not the stones
        Upon which all rests
Our joys and sorrows,
        Songs and sighs,
But do we not depend
        On one another
And our cornerstone,
Building a structure
        From end to end.

Amis,
        Frères et Soeurs
Déjà longtemps,
        Aujourd'hui
                Sans fin.

Good Morning

I love you and am
        That is in itself
        A gratitude.

Seeing you sitting there
        Every day eagerly
        Helping create together

This is the newest day
        Splendid or not
        It stands on its own

I will be thankful for it
        Unconditionally.

Recovery

(For Florence)

She took up occupancy in the guest room,
No doubt in order to have more privacy
      Of person, of thought, of soul

But to also leave the rest of us
      A household hushed,
      Controlled in blissful sleep
While she recovered.

The young student that was me
      Continued to use it as my study;
For work and projects,
Generally frenzied as only teenagers can be
      Keeping work schedules late into the night,
I was immersed in my immediateness;
      She in the wisdom of regeneration.

In a Maine Kitchen

A baby looks up
    From the depth of curious concern,
To see the cookies rising
    On a silvered sheet,
Stretching wide her arms,
"Um...um...um," she cries
    Running to hug the open door
Whose glass permits a view
    Of things to come.

Into those small arms
    Go all my baking days,
The sweetness of the gesture
    Fills me with desire;
The senses more acute to know
    The nearness of the reach,
The gentle touch,
The heart that beats for me;
    Finally teaching me
What I should know.

To innocence
    All of life is
    "Um...um...um,"
And all the beauty of her
    World is fire!

Broken Dolls

Learn to love the weakness,
    The fault,
    The habits and the traits
That build as well as destroy

Learn to accept with love

The phone cord dangling in mid-air
As the airport noise recedes.
My heart fills up the silence
    Screaming,
I can't, I won't, I don't know how.

The words slice through
    The clean white page,
The color tried out and drying,
    To form a shape,
    To express a joy, a fear.

The feeble attempts begin
    With learning to live;
To love the difference between us;
By learning to love the faults
    Within myself!

In Memoriam

Standing by the window
    Is a woman
    Weeping pity's tears;
They fall upon the sill
    Then on her hands

Staring at the night,
    Searching up and down
The endless rolling tanks,
    The rolling wheels

Caravans of trucks
    Pushing at black of night,
Silently carry their precious load;
    Boys, mere boys
Beginning life's adventures
Dreaming of the battles,
    The drama and victories
    In the offing.

Age, life and innocence
    Are looking through the window,
    Praying to be strong

Bead by bead
Row by row
She prayed as the
    Bravest of our youth
Went off to war!

Love's Labor

Waiting in the quiet apartment
    For an infrequent phone call,
    Allowed us to become sisters,
    To depend on each other;
    Mutually supportive
    As though waiting through a labor,
We endured the agony of the exasperating wait
    Throughout the long night.

Toward dawn the hours stilled,
    Air close, throats dry,
We made uncounted cups of smoky tea.

Into the light,
    The space left open
    The womb emptied,
    The heart screamed,
Tears of relief greeted the arrival.

This was a beginning
    Of so many beginnings.
I tumbled into bed,
    Knowing that the shadow of angels
Had attended this birth.

New Beginnings

Once we spoke of difficulties we might encounter
    In dealing with the "need to know" —
We acknowledged our own shortcomings
    To each other and with each other
Honesty that both shocked and stimulated us,
    Surely this is another one of the many gifts,
The new dimensions in which we find ourselves.

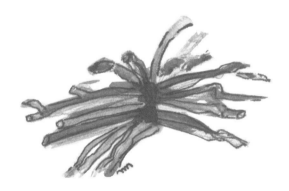